Rough Guides

25 Ultimate experiences

Britain & Ireland

Make the most of your time on Earth

ROUGH GUIDES

25 YEARS 1982–2007

NEW YORK • LONDON • DELHI

Contents

Introduction

EXPERIENCES have always been at the heart of the Rough Guide concept. A group of us began writing the books **25 years ago** (hence this celebratory mini series) and wanted to share the kind of travels we had been doing ourselves. It seems bizarre to recall that in the early 1980s, travel was very much a minority pursuit. Sure, there was a lot of tourism around, and that was reflected in the guidebooks in print, which traipsed around the established sights with scarcely a backward look at the local population and their life. We wanted to change all that: to put a country or a city's popular culture centre stage, to highlight the clubs where you could hear local music, drink with people you hadn't come on holiday with, watch the local football, join in with the festivals. And of course we wanted to push travel a bit further, inspire readers with the confidence and knowledge to break away from established routes, to find pleasure and excitement in remote islands, or desert routes, or mountain treks, or in street culture.

Twenty-five years on, that thinking seems pretty obvious: we all want to experience something real about a destination, and to seek out travel's **ultimate experiences**. Which is exactly where these **25 books** come in. They are not in any sense a new series of guidebooks. We're happy with the series that we already have in print. Instead, the **25s** are a collection of ideas, enthusiasms and inspirations: a selection of the very best things to see or do – and not just before you die, but now. Each selection is gold dust. That's the brief to our writers: there is no room here for the average, no space fillers. Pick any one of our selections and you will enrich your travelling life.

But first of all, take the time to browse. Grab a half dozen of these books and let the ideas percolate … and then begin making your plans.

Mark Ellingham
Founder & Series Editor, Rough Guides

25

Ultimate
experiences
Britain
& Ireland

1

People talk about culture vultures flocking to Edinburgh Festival, but the truth is that for an event this big you need the stamina of an ox, the appetite of a hippo and the nocturnal characteristics of an owl. The sheer scale and diversity of what's going on in the Scottish capital each August can be hard to digest properly – over half a dozen separate festivals taking place simultaneously, some 1500 different shows each day, across 200 different venues. Not to mention the street acts, the buskers, the bizarrely dressed leafleters and the simple fascination to be had just watching it all swirl around you.

Soaking up the Edinburgh Festival

How do you do the Festival without fear of disappointment or exhaustion? Book early for something significant in the International Festival, perhaps one of the world's great Philharmonic orchestras at the Usher Hall. Wander into the tented Book Festival in gracious Charlotte Square and enjoy a reading and erudite discussion with a favourite author. Take a chance on an intriguing sounding piece of theatre by a company you've never heard of in a venue you struggle to find. After all, you've scoured the reviews in the papers over a couple of cappuccinos in a pleasant café and found a four-star show you can fit in before the new film by that director you've admired for a while.

Pick up a last-minute offer on cheap tickets for a comedian you've seen do a nearly hilarious slot on telly, then join the crowds shuffling up the Royal Mile to the nightly Military Tattoo, thrilling its multinational audience with pomp, ceremony and massed pipe bands, rounded off with fireworks crashing around the castle's battlements.

Time for more? There's probably a risqué cabaret going on at one of the Fringe venues, or a crazy Hungarian folk band stomping its way into the wee small hours in a folk club. But if you're going to do it all again tomorrow, then find a quiet corner of a cosy, wood-panelled pub and order a dram of whisky. Good stuff, this culture.

need to know

The Edinburgh International Festival and much larger and less regulated Edinburgh Festival Fringe take place annually throughout August and early September, along with Film, Book, and Jazz and Blues festivals and the Military Tattoo. For more on all Edinburgh's festivals go to Ⓦ www.edinburghfestivals.co.uk.

2

GO WEST – WALKING THE
PEMBROKESHIRE COAST
PATH

The Pembrokeshire Coast Path fringes Britain's only coastal national park, which has resisted the onslaught of the 21st century in all but a few hotspots such as Tenby and St David's (and even these remain remarkably lovely). Get out and stride along part of the 299-km trail and you'll soon appreciate this evocative and spectacular edge of Wales.

Long golden surf beaches easily rival those of California; the clear green seas are the habitat of seals, whales, dolphins, sharks and, in summer, exotic species such as sunfish and even seahorses; further offshore you'll spot islands that are home to internationally important seabird colonies; you can wander atop the highest sea cliffs in Wales, bent into dramatic folds by ancient earth movements; and in the hamlets, harbours and villages you pass through along the way there are plenty of charming pubs and restaurants at which to refuel.

This variety is one of the best things about the coast path, which offers something for everyone – and not just in summer. The off-season can provide the thrilling spectacle of mighty Atlantic storms dashing ten-metre waves against the sea cliffs as you fight your way along an exhilaratingly wind-lashed beach,

whilst the next day the sun could be glittering in a clear blue sky with seabirds wheeling and screeching overhead. Take time out from your hike to relax and enjoy views across the Atlantic, which, other than the occasional lighthouse dotting the horizon, have remained unchanged since St Patrick sailed from Whitesands Beach to Ireland.

To walk the full length of the path takes up to two weeks and, surprisingly, involves more ascent than climbing Mount Everest, but even just a half-day outing along the trail is worth the effort, and acts as a reminder that Britain boasts some of the finest coastline in the world.

need to know

Pembrokeshire is some 200 miles west of London on the M4-A40 route. There are irregular train services from London Paddington and intervening stations, and no airports. Foot and bicycle are the best way to explore the region. For more info go to Ⓦ www.pcnpa.org.uk.

3
Punting on the Cam

The experienced professional punter – propelling boatloads of tourists along Cambridge's river Cam – speaks of the simple sensory pleasure to be found in the interaction of the firm riverbed, the massive pole (wielded with a masterful delicacy) and the punt itself, pushing against the springy upthrust of the gentle waters. In fact, it is like driving a people carrier with a joystick from a seat where the luggage would usually go. Your punt will naturally be attracted to other punts, blocking the river under the sarcastic gaze of the city's youth, who stop to watch your ineptitude from one of the many pretty bridges. Your response should be to affect an ironic detachment; something achieved more easily when you console yourself with the idea that perhaps punting was never meant to be done well. The point is to drift with languorous unconcern, admiring the beautiful college gardens and architecture, while disguising incompetence as abstraction and reverie.

This slow river is lined with some of the grandest architecture in the country. You recline almost at the water's level as the great buildings rear around you in a succession of noble set-pieces. Perhaps the two most notable sights are the chapel at King's College, a structure of forbidding single-minded authority, and Christopher Wren's library for Trinity College, which has the same rigorous perfection that some may find refreshing or overwhelming.

When you're done punting, the colleges are wonderful places to explore, if they'll let you in: the rules of access vary from college to college and season to season, although you can always behave as if you have a perfect right to walk wherever you like and see what happens. And finally, any visit must finish with an appraisal of the city's pubs: a favourite is the *Maypole*; low-key and a good place to unwind.

need to know

Punts can be hired from stations at Mill Lane, Magdalene Bridge and Jesus Green, and at other points along the Cam's short stretch in the city centre.
Maypole, 20a Portugal Place ☎ 01223/352 999

4 Supping **Guinness** in Dublin

Rain lashing a grey Dublin Friday. **The Palace**, etched in glass, promises refuge. In quick. No trouble catching the barman's eye, "A pint, please." As he slowly begins to pour, time to take in the handsome room: mirrored screens sectioning the bar discreetly, Victorian mahogany twirling everywhere. I eavesdrop while the half-poured Guinness stands to one side to settle: the Dublin–Mayo match on Sunday, brutal tailbacks on the M50, bin charges. More patience needed when the glass is full, waiting for the black and white turmoil to calm itself; drawings of writers Flann O'Brien and Patrick Kavanagh, old *Palace* regulars, stare down.

I settle myself in the back room, under a glass roof that floods light in and noisily reminds me of the drenching I'm missing. Clutching my pint, I think of the philosopher, struggling with the problem of consciousness, who compared beer in a glass to the brain, the mind or soul to the froth on top – same physical stuff, but in essence quite different. Surely he can't have been Irish – this dark, malty liquid seems barely on speaking terms with the creamy, white top. A twist in the tale, perhaps only possible in "God's own country": as I sup my way through the black stuff, the froth persists, sinking slowly down the glass.

Same again? A fine pint, but was it the best Guinness in Dublin – and so, I suppose, the world? Some say it's better round the corner at **Mulligan's**, where it's been sanctified by generations of Irish Times journalists. Or is the travel-shy liquid happier at **Ryan's**, just across the river from the brewery? And what about the brewery's own panoramic bar? There you get a manicured pint, as its maker intended, with views over the city and the Wicklow Mountains thrown in.

Now, what was I meant to be doing this afternoon?

need to know
The Palace, 21 Fleet St.
Mulligan's, 8 Poolbeg St.
Ryan's, 28 Parkgate St.
Guinness Storehouse, off Belleview;
Ⓦ www.guinness-storehouse.com.

Eighteenth-century Romantic poet **Thomas Gray** described the narrowest part of Borrowdale – the so-called Jaws of Borrowdale – as "a menacing ravine whose rocks might, at any time, fall and crush a traveller". Gray obviously didn't get out much, for more than anything Borrowdale is characterized by its sylvan beauty, the once glaciated hills smoothed off by the ancient ice. Some have dubbed it **the most beautiful valley in England**, and it's easy to see why on the gentle walks that weave across the flat valley floor. Some of the best are around **Derwentwater**, which with its mountain backdrop, wooded slopes and quaint ferry service is one of the prettiest lakes in the area.

Ever since Victorian times, visitors have flocked to the **Bowder Stone**, a 2000-tonne glacial erratic probably carried south from Scotland in the last Ice Age. This cube of andesitic lava is perched so precariously on one edge that it looks **ready to topple at any moment**. Wooden steps give access to its thirty-foot summit where the rock is worn smooth by hundreds of thousands of feet.

Immediately north, a circular walk takes in an area boasting the densest concentration of superb views in the Lake District. The most spectacular is from **Walla Crag** – vistas stretch over Derwentwater up to the Jaws of Borrowdale.

South of the Bowder Stone, a small tumbling stream is spanned by **Ashness Bridge**, an ancient stone-built structure designed for packhorses. With its magnificent backdrop of Derwentwater and the **rugged beauty of northern**

need to know

Borrowdale is in the heart of the Lake District, running due south of Keswick for around eight miles. Parking is limited so it pays to catch the local bus (The Borrowdale Rambler) from Keswick bus station. For accommodation, there's a YHA (Ⓦ www.yha.org.uk; £16) and several more upscale places including **Seatoller House** (☏ 017687/77218, Ⓦ www.seatollerhouse.co.uk; £52), an atmospheric seventeenth-century farmhouse.

5 Wandering Borrowdale in the Lake District

6 Be humbled in **Durham**

Durham Cathedral is now something of a celebrity to millions who've never set foot in the Northeast, having appeared as Hogwart's detention hall, courtyard and Quidditch practice arena in the Harry Potter films. This recent brush with fame, however, is a mere blink in the cathedral's centuries-old history, as Durham stands as one of the greatest and most enduring achievements of Norman architectural engineering.

Looming over this university city like a gentle giant, the cathedral offers a haven of calm from the narrow, bustling streets. Boasting the enormous lion-shaped Sanctuary door knocker that, when rapped, would guarantee desperate fugitives 37 days of refuge, the North Porch Door opens onto the broad Norman nave, flanked by immense pillars, deeply carved with geometric grooves. Lighting up the east wall of the cathedral is the magnificent Rose window, below which you'll find the final resting place of the north's popular saint, St Cuthbert, the monk from Lindisfarne famed for his healing hands, deposited here in 1104 after a protracted and somewhat unceremonious tour of the country in his coffin (he had died in 687).

A hike up the Central Tower is worth the wear on the thigh muscles; 325 steps spiral up for 67 metres, where you'll be greeted by a superb panoramic view of the surrounding county, Wearside – claustrophobics be warned: the steps are extremely steep and narrow. The entrance to the tower is in the South Transept, next to Prior Castell's colourful sixteenth-century clock, decorated with a Scottish thistle: the last remaining testament to Durham's sticky involvement in the Civil War, when Cromwell used the cathedral to imprison 3000 Scottish soldiers.

At night the Cathedral takes on an entirely new persona: bathed in artificial light, it dominates the skyline in haunting magnitude. To experience the cathedral in all its auricular glory, aim to visit around 5pm for the Evensong service, when you can enjoy the enchanting refrains of the university choristers. And if you're after more magic – this time in the culinary sense – the Almshouses café is located just across the grassy Palace Green (a perennial stage for streaking students). Sublime. The cake selection that is, not the streakers.

need to know

Situated opposite the Castle at the heart of Durham's old town, the Cathedral has free entry (suggested donation £4). Opening hours are Mon–Sat 7.30am–6pm, Sun 7.30am–5.30pm. The Tower is open Mon–Sat 10am–3pm (£3).

Covering a wedge of land between Bournemouth, Southampton and the sea, the New Forest offers some of Britain's most **exhilarating cycling country**, with a chance to lose yourself amid a network of roads, gravelled paths and bridleways, and 150 miles of car-free cycle tracks. Here, you can indulge your **wild side**, surrounded by a leafy world remote from modern-day stresses. Spring brings budding growth to the area and the ground is swathed in delicate colour, while autumn paints the forest in gorgeous hues of red and brown. Your travels will take you past tidy **thatched cottages** on quiet wooded lanes onto exposed heathland with magnificent views and dotted with deer. The 40mph speed limit on forest roads makes for a safe and unhassled ride, **picnic spots** are ubiquitous, and the occasional pub provides more substantial refreshment.

England's newest national park has been a protected wilderness for nigh on a thousand years: since **William the Conqueror** appropriated the area as a hunting reserve (his son, William Rufus, was killed here by an arrow in an apparent accident). The area has changed little since Norman times, and is a superb place to spot **wildlife**: amid terrain ranging from thick woodland to bogs, heath and grassland strewn with bracken and gorse, the forest is home to around 2000 fallow, roe, red and sika deer, not to mention some 3000 **wild ponies**, and numerous sheep, cattle, pigs and donkeys.

Park up the car, and pedal off; go fast or take your time; map out routes or ride at random – you're the boss on this invigorating **escape into freedom**.

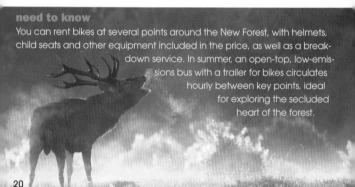

need to know

You can rent bikes at several points around the New Forest, with helmets, child seats and other equipment included in the price, as well as a break-down service. In summer, an open-top, low-emissions bus with a trailer for bikes circulates hourly between key points, ideal for exploring the secluded heart of the forest.

Cycling in the
New
Forest

7

8

See the Belfast Murals

Mention the Falls Road and Shankill districts of Belfast, and up flash images of bitter sectarian street battles between the pro-British, Protestant **Loyalists** and the Pro-Irish, largely Catholic **Republicans**.

These close neighbours have long used wall paintings to stake territorial claims, and now that Belfast is back on the tourist agenda, the murals have become star attraction.

Walking west from central Belfast to the Republican **Falls Road**, you can't miss the huge painted images adorning almost all end-terrace walls. Some are tributes to the fallen, while others commemorate specific incidents such as the 1981 prison hunger strike when Bobby Sands became a Republican martyr, along with nine comrades. Elsewhere, "Free Ireland" slogans depict wrists shackled by manacles labelled "Made in Britain". The message could hardly be clearer.

A few steps up the side streets north of the Falls Road you hit the **Peace Line**, a fortified boundary of razor wire and CCTV that separates the road from Loyalist Shankill. The heavy steel gates are now left open, hopefully permanently.

There's an altogether more militaristic feel to **Shankill**, with guns on almost every mural. Union Jacks are ubiquitous, even on the kerbstones, and one whole housing estate is ringed by red, white and blue kerbing. Most murals also bear the red hand of Ulster, which forms the centrepiece of the Ulster Flag and features on the emblems of both the UVF and UDA paramilitary organizations.

In these districts passions run high and you'd think it would feel unsettling being a rubbernecking tourist in a place that has witnessed so much bloodshed. But most people are just pleased that you're interested. If you feel at all intimidated or want a deeper insight, opt for one of the excellent **taxi tours** that visit both districts.

need to know

With suitable photo stops, walking the entire route will take three or four hours. Alternatively take a black cab such as **Big E's Belfast Taxi Tours** (℡079/6847 7924, ⓦwww.big-e-taxitours.com), which charges £25 for up to three passengers.

With surf culture currently enjoying a huge upsurge in Britain, the time is right to **wax down your board** and slip on a wetsuit. New punters and dedicated surf dudes alike are finding breaks in all kinds of unlikely places, but the Cornwall town of Newquay retains its place as capital of the **UK surf scene**. Its eleven beaches of fine sand stretching over seven miles are regularly pounded by mighty Atlantic swell, which has travelled over **3000 uninterrupted miles** to provide surfers with the kind of rides that make all the salt spray, paddling and "pearls" (tumbling off the front of the board when trying to stand up) worthwhile. It may not have the climate of Bondi, Malibu or Waikiki, but wind, tide and currents combine here to create **perfect conditions**, making Newquay the venue for regular competitions that draw visitors from Australia, the US and Japan, as well as Europe.

9
Surfing in
Newquay

Newquay's beaches **accommodate every level**: serious aficionados and intermediates head for west-facing Fistral, which has waves at all stages but is best at low tide – **beachside showers** here add to its appeal – while novices, body boarders and Malibu boarders alike will find the **sheltered beaches** of Towan, Great Western, Tolcarne and Lusty Glaze more appealing. These town beaches mostly face north or northwest and so get fewer breaks than Fistral, though a big southwest swell can pick things up considerably. When these shores get too congested for comfort, head up to Watergate Bay, home to the **Extreme Academy** (for more hardcore outdoor activities such as kitesurfing and waveskiing), a couple of **funky restaurants** and acres of empty sands. Such is the lure of surf that people come to Newquay with a bucket and spade, and **leave with a board**.

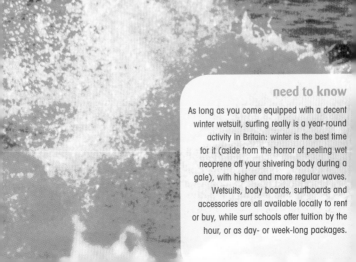

need to know

As long as you come equipped with a decent winter wetsuit, surfing really is a year-round activity in Britain: winter is the best time for it (aside from the horror of peeling wet neoprene off your shivering body during a gale), with higher and more regular waves. Wetsuits, body boards, surfboards and accessories are all available locally to rent or buy, while surf schools offer tuition by the hour, or as day- or week-long packages.

10

POST OFFICE

**Breathing in
the sea air in
Tobermory**

On the old stone fishing pier in Tobermory on the island of Mull, a very affordable indulgence is available: queue at the fish'n'chip van and order a scallop supper. It'll be served in brown paper, just like the classic (but more mundane) takeaway fish'n'chips, and you'll probably have to perch on the harbour wall to eat them, but you get a meal of steaming chips and sweet, tender scallops gathered from the surrounding waters a few hours previously, as well as free views across the prettiest port on the west coast of Scotland.

Close by, fishing boats are tied up at the pier, pyramids of lobster creels piled up in their sterns. Out in the bay yachts sit on their moorings, while large inflatable boats with deep-throated outboard engines circle near the jetty, ready to take passengers on an evening spin out to the surrounding waters to look for seals, porpoises, dolphins, basking sharks and, quite possibly, minke or killer whales.

Along the waterfront prominent tall houses are painted in vibrant blue, pink, yellow, red or gleaming white. No matter what the weather, they're an uplifting, if slightly garish, sight. The rest of the village – the grand castellated hotel, cosy guesthouses, the arts centre with its warm coffee and CDs of lilting Gaelic songs – is perched on a hillside which rises sharply up from the water. Toil up the short but steep switchback roads of the upper village and you'll be treated to increasingly impressive views of the bay, the wave-creased Sound of Mull and empty hills beyond. Venture even further, across the heathery golf course on the fringes of the village, and dramatic glimpses of the strewn islands and ragged coast to the north and west begin to appear. It's not a bad way to walk off supper.

need to know

You can get to Mull by taking the train from Glasgow to meet a ferry at the west-coast port of Oban. Once on Mull regular buses run to Tobermory. The village is the main settlement on Mull, with a good range of places to stay, eat and drink.

Though the mountains of Snowdonia rarely poke above 3000ft (914m), they exhibit a rugged majesty quite out of keeping with that statistic. This tightly packed kernel of soaring cliff faces, **jagged pinnacles** and plunging waterfalls fills a tiny corner of North Wales and yet people find enough great hiking to keep them coming back for years.

As you'd expect, the focus is on **Snowdon** itself, the highest mountain south of the Scottish Grampians. Its summit is at the apex of a grand cirque whose lofty peaks are linked by knife-edge ridges. Half a dozen well-trodden paths lead to the top, some following gentle grassy slopes, others taking increasingly intricate routes that demand good balance and a head for heights.

Snowdon is undoubtedly a fine mountain, but hardened hikers are often heard complaining about the cog railway that runs from the town of Llanberis to the café, bar and post office at the top. No matter that it's been there for a century, they'd rather hike something purer. And they don't come much purer than **Tryfan** (915m), allegedly the only mountain in Wales you can't climb without using your hands. At the blocky summit mound you'll find **Adam and Eve**, two monoliths a couple of metres high and about a metre apart. They say if you jump between them you have the **"Freedom of Tryfan"**. The jump itself is trivial, but the consequences of overshooting don't bear thinking about.

need to know

There are no fees to enter **Snowdonia National Park** or to hike any of the paths, though you may have to pay a couple of pounds for parking. Most people start from *Idwal Cottage* youth hostel, near the A5. Warm waterproof clothing is essential and compass skills are advisable. If you have any doubts, consider joining one of the residential mountain skills courses or one-day taster sessions at **Plas y Brenin** (☎01690/720214, ⓦwww.pyb.co.uk), right in the heart of Snowdonia.

Roman and Viking history, the Minster and *Betty's Tearooms* may be visitor staples during the day, but there are some rather different experiences to be had on the backstreets of York after dark. Most nights, at various points around the city, groups of tourists gather together, some nervously wringing their hands, apprehension clouding their faces, others cracking jokes. As the Minster bell tolls, the guide arrives, clad in funereal black, and a hushed silence falls upon the group. Ensuring all can hear, he leads his flock down the shadowy streets and the ghoulish journey begins. But just as you feel yourself being swept up by the guide's theatrics, one glance at the younger members of the crowd and then your wristwatch, and you are slightly reassured – it's only 7.15pm, after all.

With its turbulent history, it's not surprising that York is such a hangout for phantoms. Founded by the Romans in 71 AD as "Eboracum", the city has suffered Viking invasion, Civil War, the Black Death and a cholera epidemic. With its narrow lanes, twisting alleyways and dark, looming Tudor buildings, it's a decidedly spooky place to wander at night.

The Shambles (originally the Anglo-Saxon "Fleshammels" – meaning "Street of the Butchers") is an obligatory stop-off for any "hunting party", one of the city's oldest streets, mentioned in the Domesday Book. Ghostly apparitions that have appeared here include a headless Sir Thomas Percy, Earl of Northumberland, who was executed in 1572 for plotting against Queen Elizabeth 1; and a forlorn Margaret Clitherow, crushed to death by the authorities for illegally harbouring Catholic priests in 1586. Another stop is The Treasurer's House, reputedly the most haunted building in Britain. Legless Roman soldiers, a murderous wife and sallow-faced children are all said to lurk in the corridors of the house, built in 1419. The ghosts are not just limited to humans though: a large black hound with red glowing eyes is also said to patrol the city's gloomy snickleways and passages.

Witness to countless grim and gruesome deaths, York is a fitting location for a ghoulish hunt for things that go bump in the night.

need to know

There are six ghost hunts daily (£4), usually starting 7.15pm and lasting around an hour. Meeting points include the *Kings Arms* pub, the Minster and The Shambles. During busy periods it's best to book: contact the York Tourist Information Board (℡01904 550099, ⊛www.visityork.org).

Hunting Ghosts in York

12

It starts sometime in August, when the first of the after-party posters materialize along Ladbroke Grove and the plink-plonk rhythms of steelband rehearsals filter through the clamour of Portobello market. By the time the crowd barriers appear on street corners and the shop-owners begin covering their windows with party-scarred plywood, the feeling of anticipation is almost tangible: Carnival is coming. These familiar old streets are about to be transformed into a wash of colour, sound, movement and the pure, unadulterated joy that makes this huge street festival the highlight of London's party calendar.

Carnival Sunday morning and in streets eerily emptied of cars, sound-system guys, still bleary-eyed from the excesses of last night's warm-up parties, wire up their towering stacks of speakers, while fragrant smoke wafts from the stalls of early-bird jerk chicken chefs. And then a bassline trembles through the morning air, and the trains begin to disgorge crowds of revellers, dressed to impress and brandishing their whistles and horns. Some head straight for the sound systems, spending the entire day moving from one to the other and stopping wherever the music takes them. Streets lined by mansion blocks become canyons of sound, and all you can see is a moving sea of people, jumping and blowing whistles as wave after wave of music ripples through the air.

But the backbone of Carnival is mas, the parade of costumed bands that winds its way through the centre of the event. Crowds line up along the route and Ladbroke Grove becomes a seething throng of floats and flags, sequins and feathers, as the mas bands cruise along, their revellers dancing up a storm to the tunes bouncing from the music trucks. And for the next two days, the only thing that matters is the delicious, anarchic freedom of dancing on the London streets.

need to know

Carnival takes place on Sunday and Monday over the last bank holiday in August, from around noon to 9 or 10pm; sound systems are shut off at 7pm. For more on Carnival, visit
⊕ www.portowebbo.co.uk

THE CALL OF THE ROAD –
HITTING THE STREETS FOR
NOTTING HILL
CARNIVAL
13

14

The jagged twin pyramids of the Skellig Islands rise abruptly out of the Atlantic Ocean, 10km off the southwest tip of Ireland. **Little Skellig** is a teeming, noisy **bird sanctuary**, home to around fifty thousand gannets and now officially full (the excess have had to move to another island off County Wexford). In tranquil contrast, neighbouring **Skellig Michael** shelters one of the most remarkable **hermitages** in the world.

In the late seventh or early eighth century, a monastery was somehow built on this inhospitable outcrop, in imitation of the desert communities of the early Church fathers – and indeed, continuing the practices of Ireland's **druids**, who would spend long periods alone in the wilderness. Its design is a miracle of ingenuity and devotion. On small artificial terraces, the **dry-stone beehive huts** were ringed by sturdy outer walls, which deflected the howling winds and protected the vegetable patch made of bird droppings; channels crisscrossed the settlement to funnel rainwater into cisterns. Monks – up to fifteen of them at a time – lived here for nearly five hundred years, withstanding anything the Atlantic could throw at them – including numerous **Viking raids**. In the twelfth century, however, a climatic change made the seas even rougher, while pressure was brought to bear on old, independent monasteries such as Skellig Michael to conform, and eventually the fathers adopted the **Augustinian rule** and moved to the mainland.

The beauty of a visit to the island is that it doesn't require a huge leap to imagine how the monks might have lived. You still cross over from the mainland on small, slow boats, **huddling against the spray**. From the quay, 650 steps climb almost vertically to the monastery, whose cells, chapels and refectory remain largely intact after **1300 years**. The island even has residents, at least in the summer: friendly guides, employed by the Office of Public Works to give talks to visitors, stay out here for weeks at a time, making the most of the **spiritual solitude**.

NEED TO KNOW

Boats run out to the Skelligs, usually between May and September, from several points on the Kerry coast; operators include Sean Feehan from Ballinskelligs (☎066/947 9182, ✆www .skelligsboats.com), Brendan Casey from Portmagee (☎066/947 2437, ✆www.skelligislands .com) and Seán Murphy from Knightstown, via Reenard Point and Portmagee (☎066/947 621 ✆www.skelligislands.com). Bring walking shoes, warm, waterproof clothes, water and food.

The Balti Triangle is one of Birmingham's leading culinary assets – over fifty restaurants all competing to serve the best, simplest, no-nonsense and above all the cheapest Indian food. The apex of the fabled Triangle is where Moseley Road meets Stratford Road – two major crossroads are Highgate Road and Taunton Road – and two of the busiest balti boulevards are Ladypool Road and Stoney Lane. Balti as we know it was born in Birmingham's large Pakistani and Kashmiri communities in the 1970s and is really a testament to their business acumen rather than any fancy gastronomic impulse. As restaurateurs they saw the merits of a style of eating that linked the British love of curry with some shortcuts in the kitchen. Each dish is finished to order, so the customer always gets the combination of ingredients they want – "meat-peas-spinach" or "chicken-king prawn-extra hot". Other defining elements of balti are the use of bits torn from a huge nan bread to eat with rather than cutlery – less cutlery means less washing up; a bring-your-own-alcohol policy – less licensing hassle; and low, low prices, enabled by turning the tables at a phenomenal rate.

There are lots of restaurants to choose, but some in particular stand out; *Adil's*, founded in 1977, was one of the first balti restaurants in the country and is very traditional, even for a balti house – try the balti meat with chickpeas and extra methi. Award-winning *Al Frash* serves a deliciously spicy balti called "Afrodesia" – minced chicken and king prawn with ground ginger and garlic. *Zeb's Miripuri Cuisine* lost its frontage during a tornado in 2004 and is much smarter now, but the cooking is as good as ever – it does a mean balti chicken jalfrezi. Otherwise, just wander into the Triangle and take potluck in any restaurant that looks busy. You should expect to pay around £8 a head, and remember to take your own alcohol.

need to know

Al Frash 186 Ladypool Road ☎0121 753 3120.

Adil 148–150 Stoney Lane ☎0121 449 0335.

Zeb's Miripuri Cuisine 250 Ladypool Road ☎0121 449 8909.

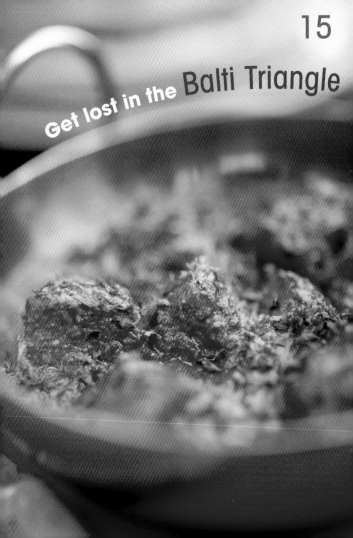

Get lost in the Balti Triangle

16 Clubbing in London

From superclubs to sweaty backrooms, hiphop to hardcore, there's a London club night guaranteed to get you throwing shapes on the dance floor. Institutions like Fabric and Ministry of Sound are pricey, but well worth it to experience world-famous DJs on knee-tremblingly loud sound systems: buy tickets in advance to avoid the three-hour queues. For a less commercial, more spontaneous vibe, keep an ear cocked for pounding basslines next time you're strolling past Festival Pier, on the South Bank. When the tide is out, free parties periodically pop up on the grubby strip of sand, attracting a diverse mix of grungy ravers and passing tourists.

North, south, east or west? Partisan local opinion is divided. In a trio of clubs hidden north amongst the industrial wasteland behind Kings Cross, a smart international crowd go mad for any kind of house music, whether funky or Ibiza euphoric. South of the river, the holy meets the hedonistic in the crypt beneath Brixton's St Matthew's Church, which hosts regular drum 'n' bass, hard tech house and trance nights. Clubbing out east veers on the theatrical, with trendy Hoxtonites striding out in vintage frocks, flat caps and dramatic make-up, as indie, pop and electro collide in weird and wonderful ways. Meanwhile, small venues and scruffy boho chic are the order of the day west in Notting Hill, with an eclectic soundtrack of soulful funk, broken beat and world music.

After-parties used to be word-of-mouth affairs, but thanks to 24-hour licensing there's now a whole host of excuses to avoid going to bed. Amongst the dedicated party people who've been out since Friday

you'll spot a fair few fresh faces who have got up on Sunday morning to go straight to a club. Whatever day of the week, there's absolutely no excuse for staying in.

need to know

Get ideas for your night out from Ⓦ www.timeout. com/london, The Guardian's *Guide* on Saturday and *One Week To Live* – a free weekly listings magazine available from independent fashion stores.

Fabric
Ⓦ www.fabriclondon.com
Ministry of Sound Ⓦ www .ministryofsound.co.uk
St Matthew's Church
Ⓦ www.babalou.net

Walking on **Dartmoor**

17

need to know

Guided walks (daily April–Sept) vary from two to six hours. Pick up a copy of the free
Visitor Guide (☎ 01822/890414) or contact the Dartmoor National Park Visitor Centre
(☎ 01822/890414, ⓦ www.dartmoor-npa.gov.uk) for further details.

In the middle of that most genteel of counties, Devon, it comes as something of a shock to encounter the 365 square miles of raw granite, barren bogland and rippling seas of heather that make up Dartmoor. The **feeling of space** is intimidating. If you want to de-clutter your mind and energize your body, the recipe is simple: invest in a pair of hiking boots, switch off your mobile and set out on an adventure into the primitive heart of Britain. The briefest of journeys onto the moor will be enough to take in the **dusky umbers** of the landscape, flecked by yellow gorse and purple heather, or the verdant patchwork of greens threaded by flashes of moorland stream, all washed in a **moist and misty light**. Even the gathering haze that precedes rain appears otherworldly, while the moor under a mantle of snow and illuminated by a crisp wintry light is spellbinding.

Your walk will take you from picturesque, hideaway hamlets such as Holne and Buckland-in-the-Moor to **bare wilderness and blasted crag** within a few strides. There are some surprising examples of architecture, too, including the authentically Norman Okehampton Castle and the wholly fake Castle Drogo, built by Lutyens in the early twentieth century in the style of a medieval fortress. But by far the most stirring manmade relics to be found are the **Bronze and Iron Age remains**, a surprising testimony to the fact that this desolate expanse once hummed with activity: easily accessible are the grand hut circles of Grimspound, where Conan Doyle set a scene from his Sherlock Holmes yarn, **The Hound of the Baskervilles**.

The best way to explore the moor is on an organized walk led by a **knowledgeable guide**, often focusing on a theme, from birdwatching to orienteering to painting. It's a first-rate way to get to grips with the terrain, and discover facets of this vast landscape which you'd never encounter on your own. Alternatively, equip yourself with a decent map and **seek out your own piece** of Dartmoor. You may not see another soul for miles, but you'll soon absorb its slow, soothing rhythm.

Even in a country as scenic as Scotland, you don't expect to combine travelling by train with classic views of the Scottish Highlands: the tracks are down in the glens, after all, tracing the lower contours of the steep-sided scenery. On the other hand, you might be craning your neck, but at least you don't have to keep your eyes on the road. And you can always get out: in fact, some of the stations on the West Highland line are so remote that no public road connects them. At each stop a handful of deerstalkers, hikers, mountain bikers, photographers or day-trippers might get on or off. It'll be a few hours until the next train comes along, but that's not a problem. There's a lot to take in.

The scenery along the West Highland Railway is both epic in its breadth and compelling in its imagery. You travel at a very sedate pace in a fairly workaday train carriage from the centre of Glasgow and its bold Victorian buildings, along the banks of the gleaming Clyde estuary, up the thickly wooded loch shores of Argyll, across the desolate heathery bogs of Rannoch Moor and deep into the grand natural architecture of the Central Highlands, their dappled birch forests fringing green slopes and mist-enveloped peaks.

After a couple of hours the train judders gently into the first of its destinations, Fort William, set at the foot of Britain's highest peak, Ben Nevis. The second leg of the journey is a gradual pull towards the Hebrides. At Glenfinnan the train glides over an impressive 21-arch viaduct most famous these days for conveying Harry Potter on the Hogwarts Express. Not long afterwards the line reaches the coast, where there are snatched glimpses of bumpy islands and silver sands, before you pull into the fishing port of Mallaig, with seagulls screeching overhead in the stiff, salty breeze, and the shape of Skye emerging from across the sea.

need to know

Trains (up to 3 daily; 5hr) run from Glasgow on the West Highland Line to Fort William and then onto Mallaig. In summer, one of the services from Fort William to Mallaig is pulled by the Jacobite steam train (Ⓦwww. steamtrain.info). Prices start at around £25 return.

18 Trundling along the West Highlands Railway

Every year in Ireland, thousands of people do the **Newgrange lottery**. Entry is by application form, with the draw made in October by local schoolchildren. And the prize? The lucky winners are invited to a bleak, wintry field in the middle of County Meath on the longest night of the year, to huddle into a dank and claustrophobic tunnel and wait for the sun to come up.

It's not just any old field, though, but part of **Brú na Boinne**, one of Europe's most important archeological sites. A slow bend in the River Boyne cradles this extraordinary ritual landscape of some forty Neolithic mounds, which served not only as graves but also as spiritual and ceremonial meeting places for the locals, **five thousand years ago**. The tunnel belongs to the most famous passage mound, Newgrange, which stretches over 75 metres in diameter, weighs **200,000 tonnes** in total and is likely to have taken forty years to build. The lottery winners get to experience the annual astronomical event for which the tomb's passage was precisely and ingeniously designed: through a roofbox over the entrance, the first rays of the rising sun on the **winter solstice** shine unerringly into the burial chamber, twenty metres away at the end of the passage in the heart of the mound.

Not everyone gets to win the lottery, of course, so throughout the year as part of an entertaining guided tour of the Newgrange mound, visitors are shown an **electrically powered simulation** of the solstice dawn in the central chamber. Once you've taken the tour and seen the impressive visitor centre at Brú na Boinne, the perfect complement is then to drive thirty kilometres west to the Loughcrew Cairns, a group of thirty similar mounds that are largely unexcavated. Here, you borrow a torch and the key to the main passage tomb, Cairn T, and you'll almost certainly have the place to yourself. With views of up to **sixteen counties** on a clear day, you can let your imagination run wild in an unspoilt and enigmatic landscape.

need to know

Served by buses from Dublin, the Brú na Boinne visitor centre (@ www.heritageireland.ie) is about 10km southwest of Drogheda, between Donore and Slane, in County Meath. The Loughcrew Cairns, about 5km southeast of Oldcastle in the northwest corner of Meath, are accessible only with your own transport – pick up the key for Cairn T (€50 deposit) and a torch at Loughcrew Gardens (@ www.loughcrew.com).

19

Winning the prehistoric lottery

"U-NI-TED!" the chant starts at the top of the Stretford End. "U-NI-TED!" the chorus engulfs the rest of the stand, rolling out around the ground. "U-NI-TED!" 70,000 voices singing as one. "U-NI-TED!" And the team hasn't even left the dressing room yet.

Watching a match at Old Trafford, Manchester United's self-styled "Theatre of Dreams", is the biggest thrill in spectator sport. The stadium (76,000 capacity) is massive, and full at every game with the Red faithful – not just from Manchester, but from all over Britain, as well as huge contingents from Ireland and Scandinavia.

They come to see a team that is truly legendary. One that, for all Chelsea's millions, or Barcelona's brilliance, remains by far the biggest name in European football. And why is that? Let's start with some history. In 1958, United lost the heart of the decade's most glorious team in the Munich Air Disaster (the clock in the South Stand still bears the fateful time) and became, overnight, a national icon. Then, ten years later, they lived the dream, becoming the first British team to win the European Cup. It was a trophy achieved with football of utter romance – forged by the great Bobby Charlton and the world's first football superstar, George Best – and the legend has never quite let up. The club lapsed for a while, but since the inauguration of the Premiership in 1992, manager Alex Ferguson's team has dominated English football, winning eight league titles, four FA Cups and, in 1999, their second European Cup, part of an unprecedented "Treble".

They have done so playing inspired, entertaining football – nothing less would be tolerated at Old Trafford. And today, as always, the inspiration comes from the wings – where Cristiano Ronaldo and Ryan Giggs ply their trickery – and from a great centre forward, Wayne Rooney, the most talented English footballer of this generation. To see this trio live, calling for the ball, racing down the pitch – it takes your breath away. Or, as the massed ranks sing, "We are the pride of all Europe, the cock of the north..."

need to know

Getting a ticket to see United at home used to be tough, but since the stadium was expanded it's become much easier. Even non-members can buy an all-in match and hotel package. Don't miss a visit to the United Museum, which is stacked with memorabilia. And combine it with a tour of Old Trafford: you get to walk down the tunnel and check out the "bling-box" in the dressing room where the stars lock up their jewellery during games. For more info on packages, the museum and tours, see Ⓦ www.manutd.com.

20
WATCHING FOOTBALL AT THE
THEATRE OF DREAMS

21

Losing yourself
in **Connemara**

On the far western edge of Europe, the **starkly beautiful** region of Connemara is a great place to get lost. Cut off from the rest of Ireland by the 40km barrier of Lough Corrib, the lie of the land at first looks simple, with two statuesque mountain ranges, the **Maam Turks** and the **Twelve Bens**, bordered by the deep fjord of Killary Harbour to the north. The coast, however, is full of jinks and tricks, a hopeless **maze of inlets**, peninsulas and small islands. Dozens of sparkling lakes and vast blanket bogs covered in purple moor grass further blur the distinction between land and water. Throw in a fickle climate, which can turn from blazing sunshine to grey, soaking mist in the time it takes to buy a loaf of bread, and the carefree sense of disorientation is complete.

This austere, infertile land was brutally depopulated by starvation, eviction and emigration during the **Great Famine of the 1840s**. Even when dramatist J.M. Synge visited in the early twentieth century, he considered any farming here to be like "the freak of an eccentric". Today, these wild and lonely margins are the ultimate fulfilment of visitors' romantic dreams of Ireland, with enough variety to warrant weeks of exploration.

Cycling on the quiet backroads – many of which were built to provide employment during the Famine – is probably the best way to get to know the area. At an even gentler pace, the outlandishly contorted geology provides **great diversity for walkers**, ranging from tough, high-level treks in the mountains to scenic hikes up isolated hummocks such as Errisbeg and Tully Hill. Connemara is also blessed with a string of beautiful, white-sand beaches, popular venues for horse riding, windsurfing and kayaking. If, after all that, you're still craving variety, you can hop over to **Inishbofin**, a picturesque island known for its warm welcome and traditional music sessions.

need to know

The *Mountains of Connemara* by Tim Robinson and Joss Lynam is a good map and guide-book for walkers, or there's *Collins Rambler's Guide: Connemara*, by Paddy Dillon. In Clifden, Connemara's main town, Walking Ireland (Ⓦ www.walkingireland.com) and Connemara Safari (Ⓦ www.walkingconnemara.com) offer walking tours. For further information about Connemara go to Ⓦ www.connemara.net or Ⓦ www.irelandwest.ie; for information about Inishbofin go to Ⓦ www.inishbofin.com.

It's not difficult to find Tate Modern. As befits a former power station, the place is huge, forbidding and boasts a 325ft chimney that towers over the most central section of the Thames. If you're a first timer, however, you need some guidance in order to get the maximum wow factor out of your initiation. You don't want to sidle up to the place from the nearest tube (Southwark), and enter via the north door. No, no, no. The right approach is crucial. Get yourself to St Paul's Cathedral, turn your back on Wren's masterpiece and head down Peter's Hill, which leads straight to the Millennium Bridge, perfectly framing the South Bank's cathedral of modern art.

The Millennium Bridge itself is a miracle of sorts: London's first new Thames crossing since Tower Bridge, and the capital's first-ever pedestrian-only bridge. Of course, its greatest claim to fame is as the "wobbly bridge". Unfortunately, the wobbling, which saw the bridge closed for nearly two years just days after its millennial opening, has now been cured, though if there's enough of you, you can always put it to the test.

Once across the river, make your way to Tate Modern's western entrance, from which a long, sloping ramp will take you into the gallery's awe-inspiring Turbine Hall. Each year the Tate commissions a colossal installation to fill this unique space, everything from a giant winter sun and ceiling mirrors to a curly matrix of over-sized playground slides. Inside the main galleries, you'll find every twentieth-century "-ism" represented, from late Impressionism and early Cubism to Abstract Expressionism and Super-Realism, and every major artist, from Monet and Picasso to Joseph Beuys and Mark Rothko. Be warned: by all means dip your feet in, but don't try to see everything at once, and leave enough time to visit the seventh-floor café (for the views).

need to know

Tate Modern is open daily 10am to 6pm (Fri & Sat until 10pm). Admission to the permanent collection is free, but there is a charge (usually around £8) for the large temporary exhibitions.

22

Take a stroll from St Paul's to Tate Modern

Is Holkham Bay in north Norfolk the **best beach in Britain**? It must certainly be the broadest. At high tide, you follow the private road from Holkham Hall, walk through a stretch of woods and expect to find the sea at your feet. But it is – literally – miles away: two miles at the very least, shimmering beyond a huge expanse of dunes, pools, flat sands and salt marsh. If it's your first visit, it may seem oddly familiar – for this was the location for Gwyneth Paltrow's walk along the sands, as Viola, at the end of **Shakespeare in Love**.

The amazing thing about Holkham is that, even with the filming of a Hollywood movie in full swing, you could have wandered onto the beach and not noticed. It is that **big**. You saunter off from the crowds near the road's end and within a few minutes you're on your own, splashing through tidal pools, picking up the odd shell, or – if it's warm enough – **diving into the sea**. You can walk along the beach all the way to Wells (to the east) or Overy Staithe (west), or drop back from the sea and follow trails through woods of **Corsican pines**. Just beware going out onto the sandbanks when there's a rising tide. It comes in alarmingly fast.

Birdlife is exceptional around Holkham – which is a protected reserve – and you'll see colonies of **Brent geese**, chattering and little terns, and many other birds. And if you head downcoast to Cley-next-the-Sea, or to Blakeney, you'll find even more riches, accompanied by rows of twitchers, camped behind binoculars. Take time to walk out to the hides at **Cley Marshes**, or for a boat ride to Blakeney Point, where you can watch up to four hundred common and grey seals basking on the mud.

need to know

The perfect place to stay is **The Victoria** at Holkham (☎ 01328 711 008, ⓦ www. holkham.co.uk; doubles from £115), at the beginning of the beach road. Book ahead and if you can't get in, at least have a meal (they've got a critically acclaimed restaurant), or a pint and barbecue. For a picnic lunch on the beach, stock up at the wonderful **Picnic Fayre** deli in Cley – packed with local cheeses, speciality breads, pies and antipasti.

23

U p on Conwy Castle battlements the wind whips around the eight solid towers that have stood on this rocky knoll for over seven hundred years. It's a superb spot with long views out across the surrounding landscape, but look down from the castle's magnificent curtain walls and you'll see all the elements that combined to make Conwy one of the most impressive fortresses of its day.

The castle occupies an important site, beside the tidal mud flats of the Conwy Estuary where pearl mussels have been harvested for centuries. To the south lie the northern peaks of Snowdonia, the mountains where the Welsh have traditionally sought refuge from invaders like the Norman English, who built this castle around 1283. Conwy formed a crucial link in Edward I's "Iron ring" of eight castles around North Wales designed to finally crush the last vestiges of Welsh resistance to his rule. Gazing upon this imposing fortress, which took just five years to build and is still largely intact, it isn't hard to understand why he was successful.

Practicalities

Conwy Castle is open daily 9.30am–5pm; £4.50, or £6.50 for joint ticket with Plas Mawr. www.cadw.wales.gov.uk.

A key part of the castle's design was its integration with the town, so that the two could support each other, and from the battlements a three-quarter-mile ring of intact town walls, 9m high and punctuated with 21 towers, loops out from the base of the castle, encircling Conwy's old town. For centuries the Welsh were forced to live outside the town walls while the English prospered within; the latter left behind a fine legacy in the form of the fourteenth-century half-timbered Aberconwy House and Plas Mawr, Britain's best-preserved Elizabethan townhouse.

Finish off the day by heading into town and walking a circuit of the thirty-foot-high town walls. Start at the very highest point (tower 13), where you get a superb view across the slate roofs of the town to the castle, and wander down towards the river where a pint on the quay outside the Liverpool Arms is de rigueur on a fine evening.

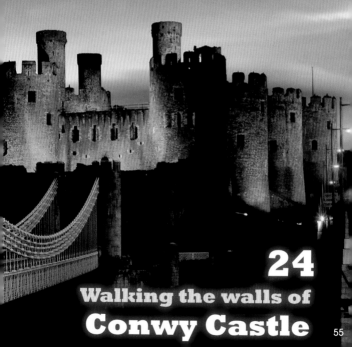

24
Walking the walls of
Conwy Castle

WE HAVE NO
MORE WELLIES

"Glastonbury" – the name conjures up so many images. It's both a place and an event; only now the latter has absorbed the mystical, mythical associations of the Glastonbury of *Arthurian and early Christian* fame – both closely entwined with the story of the Holy Grail – to become the granddaddy of all festivals. Like the legendary town of Brigadoon, it makes a brief, enchanted appearance and then it's gone, leaving a plethora of scarcely believable stories in its wake. *Did you survive Glastonbury?* Were you one of the chosen few who managed to get a ticket? (Incredibly, they are invariably sold out even before the line-up is announced.) Sure, there are bigger, brasher festivals, but Glasto is the oldest, wildest, coolest one around, where, uniquely, music makes up only part of the event. Here, *the vibe is everything* and though it attracts the biggest names – and the greatest range of acts from Bowie to REM to Rolf Harris to the English National Opera – it's what happens away from the stages that really counts. Naked fertility rites, surreal costumes, fire-dancing, yoga at dawn, and – too often – mud, *glorious mud*, exploding toilets and losing your tent. It's hippies meets rave culture; travellers meets stockbrokers; and, for the most part, smiley, happy people, and not only on account of the enormous quantities of drugs consumed. Even with the arrival of CCTV, the double perimeter fence and the watchtowers, still *the spirit lives on*. Eccentric, bolshie, comical, trans-generational, carnivalesque, there's something for everyone. You can visit the circus; listen to a stand-up show; watch Hamlet; have an Indian head massage; take a pottery class; attend a ceilidh; go shopping; watch a movie; learn to drum; *get married*, or be a guest at someone else's wedding; sleep in the dance tent; lose your friends (physically that is); and – occasionally – watch a band. It's deeply traditional, and always contemporary – like a medieval midsummer fayre with mobile phones. Arrive with *no preconceptions* and let the spirit of the festival take you. Will you survive Glastonbury?

need to know

Glastonbury takes place most years (subject to licence) at the end of June. Tickets usually go on sale in early April; Ⓦ www.glastonburyfestivals.co.uk

Ultimate experiences
Britain & Ireland
miscellany

What's in a name?

The **British Isles** is a term which encompasses the whole of England, Scotland, Wales and Ireland. **Britain** (or Great Britain if you prefer) refers only to Scotland, England and Wales. The United Kingdom (UK), on the other hand, is a political term and includes all of Britain and Northern Ireland. Eire is the official (Gaelic) term for the **Republic of Ireland** (all of Ireland, except Northern Ireland).

2 Languages

English is spoken throughout Britain and Ireland. However, Welsh is spoken by around 600,000 people, with Scottish Gaelic hanging in there with just under 60,000 speakers. Irish Gaelic is the official language of the Irish Republic (English being the second), and is understood by around 40 percent of the population, though it is the mother tongue of only around 80,000 people. In the cities across Britain and Ireland, you'll also hear an abundance of languages being spoken, with as many as **300** spoken in London.

3 Top five festivals

Edinburgh Festival The world's biggest theatre and arts festival is held every year in August in the Scottish capital.

Glastonbury Festival Started in 1970, this biennial hippy festival takes place on a farm in Somerset over the last weekend in June.

Hay Festival Britain's best-loved annual literary festival takes place in June in a tiny Welsh border town with only 1500 residents but 41 bookshops.

Notting Hill Festival Free Caribbean-inspired street party with floats and sound systems galore, held over the Bank Holiday weekend at the end of August.

St Patrick's Day Every city and town in Ireland takes the day off (March 17) to celebrate the country's patron saint, whilst in Dublin the celebrations last an entire week.

4 Richest people in Britain and Ireland

Seven out of the top ten entries in the Sunday Times Rich List 2006 for Britain are immigrants to the country. Top of the list is **Lakshmi Mittal**, an Indian steel tycoon worth nearly £15 billion; second is Roman Abramovich, the Russian oil tycoon who owns Premiership football team Chelsea, with around £11 billion; third is the Duke of Westminster with £6 billion. Harry Potter author JK Rowling is joint 122nd, and has a net worth of £520 million. The **Queen** comes in as joint 192nd, and is estimated to be worth £300m, though that's only because they don't include the Royal Collection and Palaces (which she's just looking after for the nation). The rock group U2 is thirteenth on the Irish Rich List, collectively worth £469m (€690m).

5 Five weird events

Brockworth cheese rolling Brockworth, Gloucestershire (May Bank Holiday Monday). Thousands gather to watch brave men and women hurtle down the almost vertical Cooper's Hill chasing a seven-pound cheese.

World peat-bog snorkelling championships Llanwrtyd Wells (August Bank Holiday Monday). Competitors have to complete two lengths of a 60yd peat bog trench, wearing snorkels and flippers but without using conventional swimming strokes.

Whuppity Scoorie Lanark (March 1). To usher in the spring and ward away evil spirits, the lads and lassies of Lanark chase each other round the local church beating one other with homemade paper weapons.

World Stone Skimming Championships Easdale, Argyll (last Sunday in September). This former slate mining island on the west coast of Scotland is the perfect venue for stone skimmers of the world to unite.

World Conker Championships Ashton, Northamptonshire (second Sunday in October). Modern-day gladiators fight for glory on the village green armed only with a nut and eight inches of string.

6   Top tourist attractions

Blackpool Pleasure Beach (England; 6.2 million visitors per year)
Edinburgh Castle (Scotland; 1.5 million visitors)
Guinness Storehouse, Dublin (Ireland; 750,000 visitors)
St Fagans Natural History Museum, near Cardiff (Wales; 600,000 visitors)
Giant's Causeway, Antrim (Northern Ireland; 500,000 visitors)

7   Five great films

How Green Was My Valley (1941). You can almost imagine you're in South Wales in Western director John Ford's family saga, even though he filmed it in California.

Withnail and I (1987). Bruce Robinson's mordant cult comedy is a classic 1980s period piece that moves from London via a wonderfully deserted M1 to the Lake District.

Trainspotting (1996). Witty, brilliant adaptation of Irvine Welsh's druggy novel set in an Edinburgh far from the tourist picture book.

Brief Encounter (1945). Elegant romance set in stiff-upper-lip 1940s England; a chance meeting at a train station sparks a deep but impossible love affair between two married people.

The Wind That Shakes the Barley (2006). Palm D'Or-winning drama about the Irish resistance struggle of the 1920s.

8   Kings and Queens of England

Dynasty	Monarch (Accession date)
Normandy 1066–1154	William I (William the Conqueror) (1066), William II (1087), Henry I (1100) Stephen (1135)

Plantagenet 1154–1399	Henry II (1154), Richard I (1189), John (1199), Henry III (1216), Edward I (1272), Edward II (1307), Edward III (1327), Richard II (1377)
Lancaster 1399–1461	Henry IV (1399), Henry V (1413), Henry VI (1422)
York 1461–1485	Edward IV (1461), Edward V (1483), Richard III (1483)
Tudor 1485–1558	Henry VII (1485), Henry VIII (1509), Edward VI (1547), Jane (1553), Mary I (1553), Elizabeth I (1558)
Stuart 1603–1649	James I (VI of Scotland) (1603), Charles I (1625)

In 1649 Charles I was beheaded and the **Commonwealth** declared. Oliver Cromwell became Lord Protector (1653–58) then Richard Cromwell (1658–59). The monarchy was restored in 1660.

Stuart 1660–1714	Charles II (1660), James II (VII of Scotland) (1685), William III and Mary II (1689), Anne (1702)
Hanover 1714–1901	George I (1714), George II (1727), George III (1760), George IV (1820), William IV (1830), Victoria (1837)
Saxe-Coburg-Gotha 1901–1917	Edward VII (1901), George V (1910)

George V took the name Windsor in 1917, during the First World War.

Windsor 1917–present	Edward VIII (1936), George VI (1936), Elizabeth II (1952)

9 Know your rights

A series of misguided battles in France in 1215 left King John squeezing his subjects for funding through extortionate taxes. As a result, the English barons rebelled, captured London and forced him to sign the **Magna Carta**, a series of concessions from the King guaranteeing rights and privileges for the barons. For the first time the powers of the King over his subjects were limited by a written contract. This was the initial step in a lengthy process leading to the current system of a constitutional monarchy, where the Queen remains a symbolic Head of State, but has little real power. Since 1993 she has even had to pay tax herself on her private income from the Duchy of Lancaster, though she still manages to avoid paying inheritance tax.

10 World's longest place name

Llanfairpwllgwyngyllgogerychwyrndrobwyll-llandysiliogogogoch is a town in Anglesey, North Wales. The name translates as "The Church of St Mary in the hollow of white hazel near a rapid whirlpool and the Church of St Tysilio near the red cave". However, only the first five syllables are authentic; the rest was invented in the 1880s in order to draw tourists – as indeed it has.

11 The town that came in from the cold

Berwick-upon-Tweed is the northernmost town in England – in fact, it's so far north, its football team plays in the Scottish league. A quintessential border town, it changed hands fourteen times before being finally relinquished by the Scots in 1482. An apocryphal story has it that when the Crimean War broke out against Russia in 1853, the declaration of war was signed by Queen Victoria in the name of Britain, Ireland and Berwick-upon-Tweed. However, at the end of the war the peace treaty was only signed by Britain and Ireland, meaning Berwick remained officially at war with Russia. In actual fact, Berwick wasn't mentioned in either declaration. Still, in 1966 a Soviet official put the matter to rest when he signed a peace treaty with the Mayor of Berwick.

12 Wild beasts

The most fearsome land mammal in Britain and Ireland today is the **fox**, while the largest is the **red deer**. So not much to worry about there then. Of course, the islands once boasted a much wider variety of mammals: **wolves** survived in Scotland and Ireland up until the eighteenth century, and **brown bears** and **lynxes** used to roam the countryside in pre-Roman times. More recently a semi-wild herd of **reindeer** (wiped out in the Middle Ages) has returned to the Scottish Highlands, and the **beaver** is currently being reintroduced to Argyll. Although lynxes were last seen in the British Isles approximately two thousand years ago, many people believe there are still big cats roaming the wild in Britain. The most notorious is the so-called **Beast of Bodmin Moor**, a black, panther-like creature which reputedly lives in Cornwall.

13 Religion

▶▶ Population of Britain by religion according to census forms completed in 2001

Religion	Number (percentage of population)
Christian	41,014,811 (71.6)
Muslim	1,588,890 (2.7)
Hindu	558,342 (1.0)
Jedi Knight *	390,000 (0.6)
Sikh	336,179 (0.6)
Jewish	267,373 (0.5)
Buddhist	149,157 (0.3)
Other	159,167(0.3)
No religion	8,596,488 (15.1)
Religion not stated	4,289,520 (7.3)

* Included in the category: No religion

14 Music

▸▸ Summer music festivals

Barely a week goes by over the summer months when there isn't some sort of outdoor shindig going on. The big names – **Reading** and **Leeds** (now known jointly as the Carling Weekend), and relative newcomers such as Scotland's **T in the Park** and the two **V** events – tend to draw the largest crowds and most currently favoured acts, while other mid-sized newbies such as the revived **Isle of Wight Festival** and its late-season Isle of Wight brother, **Bestival**, fill in the gaps. August's **The Big Chill** is, as you might expect, a more laid-back, family-orientated affair. Then there's the niche and specialist dos, including Reading's well-established world-music extravaganza, **WOMAD**, and the notoriously hard-to-get-tickets-to **Cambridge Folk Festival**, both held in July; others include **Creamfields** – house and diehard dance fans only; and the **Brecon Jazz Festival** for cool jazz sounds.

Bestival Robin Hill Country Park, Newport, Wales
Brecon Jazz Festival Brecon, Powys, Wales
Cambridge Folk Festival Cherry Hinton Hall Grounds, Cambridge, England
Carling Weekend Reading Rivermead Leisure Complex, Reading, England; Leeds Bramham Park, Leeds, England
Creamfields Daresbury Easte, Halton, Cheshire, England
Isle of Wight Fesitval Seaclose Park, Newport, Wales
T in the Park Balado, near Kinross, Scotland
The Big Chill Eastnor Castle, Ledbury, England
V Hylands Park, Chelmsford, England; Weston Park, Staffordshire, England
WOMAD Rivermead Leisure Complex, Reading, England

15 Places to stay

▸▸ Five stylish hotels

Hotel du Vin, Brighton Contemporary hotel with luxuriously furnished rooms and a fantastic bar. ⦿ www.hotelduvin.com.

St Brides Hotel, Pembrokeshire Stylish spa hotel set in an ideal cliff-top location in southwest Wales, with a gallery featuring Welsh contemporary art. ⓦwww.stbrideshotel.com.

The Merchant Hotel, Belfast Five-star luxury in the heart of Belfast city centre. Twenty-six opulently furnished rooms located in a Grade A-listed building. ⓦwww.themerchanthotel.com.

The Witchery by the Castle, Edinburgh Intimate hotel, featuring seven suites kitted out Gothic-style in antique furniture and tapestry drapes, with an equally indulgent restaurant. ⓦwww.thewitchery.com.

The Sanderson, London Favoured haunt of celebrities, with bright white rooms and all the luxuries you'd expect. If you can't afford to stay the night, just stop for a drink in the *Long Bar*. ⓦwww.sandersonhotel.com.

▸▸ Five luxurious country retreats

Babington House, Somerset Trendy country house hotel set in acres of impressive grounds, and featuring a bar, restaurant, cinema, pool room and a spa. ⓦwww.babingtonhouse.co.uk.

Dalhousie Castle, Midlothian, Scotland Historic thirteenth-century castle where guests can dine in the *Dungeon Restaurant*, and handle hawks and owls in the Falconry. ⓦwww.dalhousiecastle.co.uk.

The Devonshire Arms, Skipton Luxurious country retreat, occupying an old coaching house in the heart of the beautiful Yorkshire Dales. ⓦwww.thedevonshirearms.co.uk.

St Ervan Manor, Padstow, Cornwall Luxurious B&B with an elegant restaurant situated in a nineteenth-century Grade II-listed building. ⓦwww.stervanmanor.co.uk.

Ballymaloe House, nr Cork, Ireland Charming family-run country house hotel set on a 200-acre farm that is just as famous for its award-winning restaurant. ⓦwww.ballymaloe.ie.

16 The National Health Service

The **NHS**, which was set up in the 1948 to run the UK's public hospitals and health clinics, is the third biggest employer in the world, after the Chinese army and the Indian State Railways, employing four percent of the working population in England alone.

17 Government

The UK is a **parliamentary democracy**, with the Queen as head of state. Ireland, on the other hand, is a **Republic** with a popularly elected president as head of state. The UK parliament in Westminster, London, is divided into two: the House of Commons where members of parliament (MPs), voted for by the people, do their work; and the House of Lords, peopled by superannuated Lords and Ladies appointed by successive prime ministers, plus 92 hereditary peers, 26 Church of England bishops and archbishops, appointed by the Queen, and the Law Lords. Scotland has its own parliament in Holyrood, Edinburgh, with 129 elected MSPs; the parliament has only limited control over taxes and no say on foreign policy. Wales also has its own assembly in Cardiff, with 60 members (AMs or ACs), the majority of whom are women; the assembly has no tax-collecting powers. As in the UK, the Irish parliament is divided into two: the Dáil, where the elected members of parliament (TDs) and the Taoiseach (prime minister) work; and the Seanad, whose members are appointed by various organizations.

18 Literature

▸▸ Five great reads

Great Expectations, Charles Dickens
Semi-autobiographical tale of a young orphan boy who unexpectedly comes into money. With an array of larger-than-life characters, the story moves from the wind-swept marshes of Kent to the excitement and bustle of London.

Dubliners, James Joyce
Fifteen sharply drawn and sometimes poignant stories evoking the rich variety of the Irish capital and its inhabitants at the beginning of the twentieth century.

To the Lighthouse, Virginia Woolf
A family holiday in Scotland is the starting point for this experimental novel, which explores the nature of time, aspiration and personal relationships in vivid and poetic language.

The Prime of Miss Jean Brodie, Muriel Spark

Set in an Edinburgh school in the 1930s, this witty novel is centred around the influence – benign and otherwise – of charismatic teacher Jean Brodie on her most favoured pupils.

Collected Stories, Dylan Thomas

Wales's most famous poet was also an occasional writer of prose. This collection gathers up his best pieces, including *A Child's Christmas in Wales* and *Quite Early One Morning*, which he later turned into his famous radio play *Under Milk Wood*.

19 **Superstitions**

Many British and Irish people hold **common superstitions** such as touching wood for good luck, never walking under ladders or opening an umbrella indoors, or twisting an apple stalk to determine the initial of the person you are going to marry, but some old superstitions haven't survived, including:

• A new moon seen over the right shoulder was believed to be lucky, seen over the left was unlucky and seen straight ahead meant good luck to the end of the month.

• If you accidentally left the lid off the pot when making tea, it meant a stranger was going to visit.

• The herb rosemary was believed to grow best in the garden of families where the woman was in charge.

• To know the name of the person you were destined to marry, you should put a snail on a plate of flour, cover it and leave it overnight; in the morning the initial letter of the name would be traced in the flour.

• A cure for whooping cough could be found by asking a rider of a piebald horse to recommend a course of action, and then strictly following his instructions.

20 **Britain's shortest war**

In 1896, when the sultan of British-controlled Zanzibar died, his second son seized the throne and declared himself sultan, supported by Germany. Britain, concerned they would lose control of the island to Germany, demanded he step down. Needless to say he didn't, and at

9am on August 27, Britain declared war and began bombarding the island. With no effective means of defence, the sultan surrendered 45 minutes later.

21 Ten discoveries and inventions

Telephone: Alexander Graham Bell in 1876
Penicillin: Alexander Fleming in 1928
Locomotive: George Stephenson in 1829
DNA: Francis Crick and James D Watson in 1953
Electron: by Joseph John Thomson in 1897
Vaccination: Edward Jenner in 1796
Electromagnets: William Sturgeon in 1825
World Wide Web: Tim Berners-Lee in 1990
Television: John Logie Baird in 1925
Catseye road studs: Percy Shaw in England in 1934
The Lava Lamp: Edward Craven Walker in 1963
Dolly the Sheep: Keith Campbell in 1996

22 Five celebrity chef-owned restaurants

Fifteen, London Jamie Oliver. Jamie's flagship enterprise takes on unemployed kids to train as chefs who wouldn't normally get a chance to do so – and it works. Trattoria-style food. ⓦ www.fifteenrestaurant.com.

The Seafood Restaurant, Padstow Rick Stein. Rick may monopolize the eating establishments in this Cornish seaside town, but *The Seafood Restaurant* is considered one of Britain's best places to eat fish. ⓦ www. rickstein.com.

Le Manoir aux Quat' Saisons Raymond Blanc. Exquisite modern French cuisine at this two-Michelin-starred Manor House hotel and restaurant near Oxford. ⓦ www.manoir.com.

Restaurant Gordon Ramsay, London Gordon Ramsay. This Chelsea restaurant is a class act through and through; not surprisingly you have to book well in advance. ⓦ www.gordonramsay.com.

The Fat Duck, Bray Heston Blumenthal. Famous for his adventurous tasting menu, which features unusual combinations such as egg and bacon ice cream, Blumenthal's culinary explorations have resulted in his restaurant being awarded three Michelin stars. ⓦ www.fatduck.co.uk.

23 Sport

In June 2005 darts was recognised as a sport by all four of the UK's sports councils. Supporting information given in the British Darts Organization's application included the fact that during one tournament, the England captain Martin Adams walked over 25 kilometres during practice and matchplay.

▸▸ Ten most popular sports

Football
Rugby
Cricket
Tennis
Golf
Horse racing
Rowing
Hockey
Hurling
Shinty

24 Five classical composers

William Byrd (c.1537–1623). A contemporary of Shakespeare, Byrd was arguably the greatest composer in what was a golden age for English music.

Most famous works: *Ave Verum* and *Mass for Four Voices*.

Henry Purcell (1659–95). Henry managed to cram a lot of music into his brief career as organist at Westminster Abbey and as a favoured court composer.

Most famous works: *Funeral Music for Queen Mary* and *Dido and Aeneas*.

George Frederick Handel (1685–1759). A German from Saxony, Handel spent most of his working life in England writing operas and oratorios – a form he virtually invented.

Most famous works: *The Water Music, Julius Caesar* and *Messiah*.

Edward Elgar (1857–1934). With their combination of exuberance and melancholy, Elgar's orchestral and choral works are, for many, the epitome of Englishness.

Most famous works: *Pomp and Circumstance March No.1, Cello Concerto* and *Symphony No.1*.

Benjamin Britten (1913–76). Britain's most celebrated composer of modern times wrote music of an austere beauty. He was a particularly gifted setter of English poetry.

Most famous works: *Serenade for Tenor, Horn and Strings, Peter Grimes, The War Requiem*.

25 Laws

Britain possess a long and rich history that stretches back over hundreds of years, and many of the laws that exist today date back just as far; though, sadly, they are rarely upheld:

• It is illegal to enter the Houses of Parliament dressed in a suit of armour.

• By law, all London taxi drivers must ask their passengers if they have small pox or the plague.

• A law passed in 1366 forbids English people from marrying Irish people.

• If a dead whale is found anywhere on the British coast the tail belongs to the Queen, in case she needs the bones for a new corset.

Ultimate experiences
Britain & Ireland
small print

Britain & Ireland
The complete experience

ROUGH GUIDES – don't just travel

We hope you've been inspired by the experiences in this book. To us, they sum up what makes Britain and Ireland such extraordinary and stimulating places to travel. There are 24 other books in the 25 Ultimate Experiences series, each conceived to whet your appetite for travel and for everything the world has to offer. As well as covering the globe, the 25s series also includes books on **Journeys, World Food, Adventure Travel, Places to Stay, Ethical Travel, Wildlife Adventures** and **Wonders of the World**.

When you start planning your trip, Rough Guides' new-look guides, maps and phrasebooks are the ultimate companions. For 25 years we've been refining what makes a good guidebook and we now include more colour photos and more information – on average 50% more pages – than any of our competitors. Just look for the sky-blue spines.

Rough Guides don't just travel – we also believe in getting the most out of life without a passport. Since the publication of the bestselling Rough Guides to **The Internet** and **World Music**, we've brought out a wide range of lively and authoritative guides on everything from **Climate Change** to **Hip-Hop**, from **MySpace** to **Film Noir** and from **The Brain** to **The Rolling Stones**.

Publishing information

**Rough Guide 25 Ultimate experiences
Britain & Ireland** Published May 2007
by Rough Guides Ltd, 80 Strand, London
WC2R 0RL
345 Hudson St, 4th Floor, New York, NY
10014, USA
14 Local Shopping Centre, Panchsheel
Park, New Delhi 110017, India
Distributed by the Penguin Group
Penguin Books Ltd,
80 Strand, London WC2R 0RL
Penguin Group (USA)
375 Hudson Street, NY 10014, USA
Penguin Group (Australia)
250 Camberwell Road, Camberwell,
Victoria 3124, Australia
Penguin Books Canada Ltd,
10 Alcorn Avenue, Toronto, Ontario,
Canada M4V 1E4
Penguin Group (NZ)
67 Apollo Drive, Mairangi Bay, Auckland
1310, New Zealand
Printed in China
© Rough Guides 2007
80pp
A catalogue record for this book is
available from the British Library
ISBN: 978-1-84353-816-5
The publishers and authors have done
their best to ensure the accuracy and
currency of all the information in **Rough
Guide 25 Ultimate experiences Britain
& Ireland**, however, they can accept
no responsibility for any loss, injury, or
inconvenience sustained by any traveller
as a result of information or advice
contained in the guide.

1   3   5   7   9   8   6   4   2

Rough Guide credits

Editor: Karoline Densley
Design & picture research: Dan May
Cartography: Katie Lloyd-Jones, Maxine
Repath

Cover design: Diana Jarvis, Chloë
Roberts
Production: Aimee Hampson, Katherine
Owers
Proofreader: Kate Berens

The authors

Donald Reid (Experiences 1, 10, 18) is the co-author of the Rough Guides to Britain, Scotland, Scottish Highlands & Islands and author of Edinburgh Directions. **Alf Alderson** (Experience 2) lives in Pembrokeshire and is a Rough Guides author. **Nick Jones** (Experience 3) is a freelance writer, and honed his punting skills while studying at Cambridge. **Paul Gray** (Experiences 4, 14, 19, 21) is the co-author of the Rough Guide to Ireland and Dublin Directions. **Paul Whitfield** (Experiences 5, 8, 11, 24) is the co-author of the Rough Guides to Britain and Wales. **Lucy White** (Experiences 6, 12) is a Rough Guide editor and studied at Durham University, and has spent many a night being spooked in York. **Robert Andrews** (Experiences 7, 9, 17, 25) is the author of the Rough Guide to Devon and Cornwall. **Polly Thomas** (Experience 13) was born and

brought up in west London, and has attended Notting Hill Carnival since she was knee-high to a grasshopper. **Charles Campion** (Experience 15) is a freelance food writer and critic, and has written a number of Rough Guides. **Melanie Kramers** (Experience 16) lives in London and can be found most nights in a club till the early hours of the morning. **Keith Drew** (Experience 20) is an editor and sports hack. Most of the time he's a dyed-in-the-wool Fulham fan. **Rob Humphreys** (Experience 22 and Miscellany) is the author of the Rough Guide to London, and co-author of the Rough Guides to Britain, Scotland and Scottish Highlands and Islands. **Mark Ellingham** (Experience 23) is the founder of Rough Guides and regularly visits the north Norfolk coast. **Emma Kirby** (Miscellany) is a freelance journalist.

Picture credits

Cover Hiker on Dartmoor © Graham Gough/
www.britainonview.com
2 Windbreaker, Holkham beach © Rod
Edwards/www.britainonview.com
6 Red stag deer, New Forest © David Norton/
Alamy
8–9 Royal Mile, Edinburgh © Stephen
Whitehorn/DK Images; festival tightrope walker
© Helena Smith/Rough Guides; festival street
performer © Mark Thomas; festival fire juggler ©
Paul Harris/DK Images; festival posters © Helena
Smith/Rough Guides
10–11 Freshwater West, Pembrokeshire Coast
National Park © CW Images/Alamy
12–13 Punting on the River Cam © Ingrid
Rasmussen/www.britainonview.com
14–15 Pint of Guinness © Mark Thomas;
musicians in pub © David Sanger/Alamy
16–17 Hiker on Borrowdale © Alamy;
Borrowdale hills © Tom Mackie/Alamy
18–19 Durham Cathedral © Joe Cornish/DK
Images; stained glass © Joe Cornish/DK Images
20–21 Red stag deer, New Forest © David
Norton/Alamy; cyclist in the New Forest ©
istockphoto
22–23 UDA mural, Belfast © Arco Images/Alamy
24–25 Newquay surfer © Alamy
26–27 Tobermory post office © Rod Edwards/
www.britainonview.com
28–29 Adam and Eve, Snowdonia © Colin
Woods/Alamy
30–31 The Shambles, York © McCormick-
McAdam/www.britainonview.com; York
gargoyle © Joe Cornish/DK Images
32–33 Man at Notting Hill Carnival © Karolina
Krasuska/Everynight Images; costume parade,
Notting Hill Carnival © Earl Patrick Lichfield/
www.britainonview.com; carnival dancer ©
Demetrio Carrasco/Rough Guides
34–35 Skellig islands © David Lyons/Alamy
36–37 Balti dish © Sparky/Getty
38–39 Dancer in mask © Bangface; Reclaim
the Beach, Waterloo Pier © Dubversion; dancer
at Reclaim the Beach © Dubversion; London
club dancer © Naki/PYMCA; dancer in green
light © istockphoto; crowd at Fabric © David
Swindells/PYMCA
40–41 Cross and purple heather on Dartmoor ©
Philip Fenton/www.britainonview.com
42–43 West Highland Railway © Rod Edwards/
www.britainonview.com
44–45 Exterior view of Newgrange © Geray
Sweeney/Corbis
46–47 Premier League match: Manchester
United v Chelsea © Christian Liewig/Liewig
Media Sports/Corbis
48–49 Boat at Ballynahinch, Connemara ©
Kevin Galvin/Alamy
50–51 Millennium Bridge and Tate Modern © DK
Images; sun installation by Olafur Eliasson, Tate
Modern © Eva-Lotta Jansson/Corbis
52–53 Windbreaker on Holkham beach, Norfolk
© Rod Edwards/www.britainonview.com
54–55 Conwy Castle and walls © Images Etc
Ltd/Alamy
56–57 Men in costumes © urban75.com;
festival-goers in mud © urban75.com; fire
dancers © urban75.com; festival stall sign ©
urban75.com; Green Fields © Mark Thomas;
hippies © Ian Tyas/Getty Images; crowd
watching band on stage © Matt Candy/Getty
Images
58 Borrowdale hills © Tom Mackie/Alamy

ROUGH GUIDES

New Zealand

Budapest

Thailand

Greece

Punk

Italy

India

Over 70 reference books and hundreds of travel
guides, maps & phrasebooks that cover the worl